THIS MAN IS GOOD NEWS

– A newsman reports on Jesus Christ

This Man is Good News

– A newsman reports on Jesus Christ

LOUIS CASSELS

LUTTERWORTH PRESS
GUILDFORD AND LONDON

First published in Great Britain 1974

First published in the U.S.A. under the title of THIS FELLOW JESUS by Warner Press Inc, 1200 East 5th Street, Anderson, Indiana 46011, U.S.A.

ISBN 0 7188 2104 1

Printed in Great Britain by
Cox & Wyman Ltd, London,
Reading and Fakenham

CONTENTS

All biblical quotations are taken from GOOD NEWS FOR MODERN MAN, *Today's English Version* of the New Testament by permission of the publishers, William Collins, Sons & Co. Ltd.

What do we really know about Jesus?
Can his words bring hope to faltering hearts?

Louis Cassels, a senior editor of United Press International asks – and answers – questions that disturb many men and women about Jesus.

How reliable are the Gospels as a history of actual events? What can a modern science-orientated person believe about the Resurrection? What about the Virgin Birth? How authentic are the 'miracles'. What did he say about adultery, forgiveness, tolerance, justice – and especially about love? Was his world at all like ours? How can an obscure itinerant preacher who lived 2,000 years ago say anything relevant to us today?

If you have ever asked yourself these questions; if you have secretly wondered whether your faith was false or foolish – read this extraordinary book.

To the beautiful and brilliant lady who types my manuscripts, prepares my meals, soothes my sorrows and enlivens with her company every day of my life.

CHAPTER ONE

The man we should have forgotten

A college student once said to me:

'I would like to believe the things Christians believe about Jesus. But I find the story incredible.'

'Tell me,' I replied, 'which detail of the biblical record of Jesus' life do you find more improbable than the fact that you and I are talking about him, debating who he was and what his life signified, 2,000 years after he was executed as a criminal in an obscure province of the Roman Empire?'

He agreed, after reflection, that this is indeed the strangest aspect of the Jesus story – the simple, obvious and indisputable fact that he continues generation after generation to be an object of intense interest to people of all ages, races, nations, cultures and levels of intelligence.

Jesus spent his entire life in an area smaller than Wales. Until he was about thirty years old, he earned a living as a carpenter in a dusty little village named Nazareth, nestled in the Galilean hills about twenty miles from the Mediterranean sea in the sparsely populated southern part of Roman-occupied Palestine.

Then for a very brief period – no longer than three years and quite possibly only one year – he set forth on a new career as an itinerant preacher. His travels were largely confined to the rural province of Galilee. Only in the last week of his life did he venture into the capital city of Jerusalem. If you could gather together in one place all of the people who ever heard him speak, they wouldn't begin to fill a modern football stadium.

The religious leaders and political authorities who constituted The Establishment of Palestine had heard disturbing rumours of a young preacher who was 'stirring up the people' in Galilee. When he finally arrived in Jerusalem, they saw for themselves that he was becoming a popular hero – and they heard first-hand his 'radical' and 'heretical' teaching.

So they decided, with that bland disregard for individual rights which is the hallmark of all well-established Establishments, that they'd better get rid of this troublemaker. They acted fast. Within a week of his appearance in the capital, they had (1) bribed one of his followers to betray him; (2) rigged a phony trial to frame him on sedition charges; and (3) put him to death by the most agonizing form of execution ever devised by the Romans – crucifixion.

His little band of disciples, who had followed him to Jerusalem, fled in panic back to their native Galilee and went into hiding.

By all the laws of historical logic, the story should end right there – and you and I should never have heard a word of it. Jesus *should* have been quickly forgotten, even in the Galilean villages where people once gathered to hear him speak.

But he *hasn't* been forgotten – and that is an historical fact so utterly implausible that any open-minded person should be prepared to consider extraordinary explanations of it.

Here we are, twenty centuries later and thousands of miles away, living in an urban civilization which already is bored with such feats as sending men to the moon, and still we remain fascinated by this Jewish carpenter from Nazareth. Our attitudes towards him vary. Some are openly hostile towards him, and write books trying to put him down as a fraud. Others admire him on the basis of a vague knowledge of what he did and said, and gladly accord him the respect due to one of the greatest moral teachers of history, on a par with Socrates, Buddha and Confucius. Still others worship him, call him Lord, and equate him with God – a risky reverence, for if unwarranted it surely is idolatrous.

You will soon discover, as you read this book, which point of view I hold. But I promise you I won't try to ram my viewpoint down your throat or stack the evidence to con you into accepting it. I am not a theologian but a press agency reporter, and I am too steeped in the press agency tradition of telling the facts as truthfully as possible to have any stomach for the role of propagandist.

Besides, I don't think Jesus would want any high-pressure brainwashing attempted in his name. He never used spellbinding techniques of oratory in his own preaching. His whole approach was to be reasonable, to appeal to the everyday experience and common sense of his listeners. In fact, his favourite method of teaching was to tell a story, leaving the listener to draw his own conclusions about the point.

That's what I'm going to do in this little book – tell

you the story of Jesus, and let you draw your own conclusions. I'll tell you frankly what I think but I'll also try to be fair in presenting reasons why others have different views.

Then you can decide for yourself which is more difficult for a rational person of our time: to accept the mind-boggling claims Christians make for Jesus, or to account for his impact on history *without* acknowledging that he was a most extraordinary person.

CHAPTER TWO

Fact or fiction

Two facts about Jesus, which were long in dispute among scholars, have been established in recent years beyond reasonable doubt.

The first is that he was a real person, not a mythical figure. He lived and loved, worked and worried, suffered and died in a particular place, Palestine, at a particular time in history, about 2,000 years ago.

This is now conceded even by the official Institute of Militant Atheism in Soviet Russia, which has been engaged for more than forty years in a futile attempt to stamp out the religious faith that Karl Marx called 'the opiate of the people'.

The Institute was the last to abandon the once-popular hypothesis that Jesus was just a mythical figure like Jupiter, Beowulf or Robin Hood. Less-biased scholars had long since reached the same conclusion. 'No reputable historian today doubts the evidence of Jesus,' says Professor John Knox, a leading New Testament scholar. 'The question of historicity has been answered on grounds as solid and objective as anyone could want.'

The second fact which contemporary research has established, to a far greater degree than many thought possible, is that we know quite a lot about this fellow

Jesus, even though he lived long ago and far away, and was in his lifetime an obscure travelling preacher rather than a king or satrap.

Most of what we know about Jesus comes from the written records and oral traditions handed down by his original followers, who were known, in accordance with the Jewish custom of that era, as his disciples.

But there are also descriptions of Jesus and his career in secular histories of the period, written by non-Christians who cannot be suspected of any propaganda bias. The most important of these, perhaps, is a passage found in Volume 18 of a massive historical work called *Jewish Antiquities* by the Jewish-Roman historian Flavius Josephus, who was born in Jerusalem about A.D. 37. Many scholars doubted the authenticity of the Josephus passage until recently, because it seemed to accept, without question, the Christian beliefs that Jesus was divine, that he rose from the dead, and that he was the true Messiah.

It was suspected that some Christian scribe, who felt that piety took precedence over his professional duty to make an accurate copy of an ancient Greek text, had interpolated Christian dogma into whatever Josephus originally wrote about Jesus.

This thesis was documented in 1972 by a famous Jewish scholar, Professor Shlomo Pines, of Hebrew University in Jerusalem. The professor found an old Arabic translation of Josephus' history, on which no Christian scribe had laid editorial hands. Here is what it says about Jesus:

'At this time there was a wise man who was called Jesus. And his conduct was good, and he was known to be virtuous. And many people from the Jews and other nations became his disciples.

'Pilate condemned him to be crucified and to die. And those who had become his disciples did not abandon his discipleship. They reported that he had appeared to them three days after his crucifixion and that he was alive; accordingly, he was perhaps the Messiah concerning whom the prophets have recounted wonders.'

Now *that* version sounds to scholars – and to this newspaper reporter – like something a secular historian of Jewish-Roman background actually would have written about events he did not witness first-hand but of which he had heard, because they caused quite a stir in first-century Jerusalem. Note that even the sceptical historian – while carefully attributing to Jesus' disciples the story of the resurrection – is willing to concede that this extraordinary man 'was perhaps the Messiah'.

There are other non-Christian records of Jesus, including a cryptic passage in the Talmud which speaks of his having been put to death 'on the eve of the Passover' because he 'enticed Israel to apostasy'.

But we are mainly dependent on the New Testament, and particularly its four 'Gospels',* for detailed knowledge of the life and activities of Jesus.

How reliable are the Gospels as a history of events that really happened? That question has agitated Christian scholarship for nearly two centuries. Strong scepticism about the validity of many details of the Gospel story originated in German universities – the foun-

* The term 'gospel' is derived from a Middle English word, 'godspell', which means 'good news'.

tainhead of so many theological fads – in the Nineteenth Century. It was based on the assumption that the Gospels were written many years after Jesus lived, and that their core of authentic remembrance had been overlaid with the kind of myth and legend that grows up, with the passage of time, around any powerful personality (as witness, for example, the entirely baseless cherry tree tale about George Washington).

Textual analysis of the New Testament, designed to 'retrieve the kernels of fact from the husks of myth', came to be known as form criticism. It achieved a great vogue in Germany and was belatedly imported to American seminaries. One of its best-known exponents was Dr Albert Schweitzer, who concluded in his famous book, *Quest of the Historical Jesus*, that it was impossible at this remove in time to be sure of anything about the Jesus of history. Schweitzer's solution was to abandon scholarship and go to Lambarene, Africa, to heal the sick as a servant of the risen Lord Christ, whom he felt he did know intimately.

Form criticism reached its height with the work of the German theologian Rudolph Bultmann, who argued that the Gospels could be meaningful to modern man only if they were rigorously 'de-mythologized' – i.e. stripped of all supernatural elements. These Bultmann simply wrote off, without particularly arguing the point, as being obvious mythical accretions.

Tons of books and monographs were published in the nineteenth century and during the first seventy years of this century to bolster Bultmannism. Nearly every line of every Gospel was nit-picked by some aspirant doctor of theology until the average pastor and layman began to wonder whether *anything* in the New Testament was believable. And the question was a sound one: Had the Gospels been as riddled with lies as Bultmann and company contended in their heyday, there really wouldn't have been much point in taking seriously what was left over.

But Bultmannism has had its day. Three things helped to pull the plug on it. The first was a revolt by Bultmann's own ablest students, including Gunther Bornkamm, who decided that their master had pushed his thesis far too far. In his great book, *Jesus of Nazareth* (Harper and Row, 1960), Bornkamm says there is no reason to despair of knowing the real Jesus through the Gospels. On the contrary, 'the Gospels bring before our eyes ... the historical person of Jesus with the utmost vividness. Quite clearly what the Gospels report concerning the message, the deeds and the history of Jesus is distinguished by an authenticity, a freshness, and a distinctiveness not in any way affected by the Church's Easter faith. They point us directly to the earthly figure of Jesus.'

The second nail was driven into the intellectual coffin of extreme biblical criticism by scholars such as Will Herberg and Peter Berger, who pointed out that it is fully as naïve for our generation to dismiss the supernatural out of hand, just because it is not congenial to our 'scientific' preconceptions, as it was for the people of the Middle Ages to accept supernatural explanations for everything they couldn't readily understand. This overdue observation fell on fertile soil, for the best young minds of the contemporary generation already had sensed, more or less intuitively, that Hamlet was right: 'There are more things between heaven and earth, Horatio, than are dreamt of in your philosophy.' The student generation's revolt against materialism and its inevitable concomitant, meaninglessness of life, has been expressed in many forms, ranging from the Jesus movement to a sharply revived interest in ESP, spiritualism, and the so-called 'occult arts'. Not many years ago, the hallmark of a university-educated intellectual was his stoic assumption that there is nothing more to life than such phenomena as may result from accidental collocations and collisions of atoms created and guided by random chance. Today, relatively few intellectuals – including leading scientists – would consider this an adequate philosophy of life. There has to be something *beyond* nature for nature itself to make sense.

But the most exciting new corroboration of the historical validity of the Gospels is the contribution not of theology nor of philosophy, but of archaeology. In 1947, wandering Bedouins discovered, in dry caves near the Dead Sea in northern Israel, the remarkably well preserved remains of what once was an extensive library, probably belonging to a monastery of the Jewish sect of Essenes. The late Edmund Wilson, a great literary critic whose expertise in the theological area was minuscule, rushed into print in *The New Yorker* magazine with a sensational article contending that the Dead Sea Scrolls would invalidate Christianity by showing that many of its supposedly original beliefs and practices were borrowed from the Essenes.

Actually, Wilson was about as wrong as a man can be. The Essene 'Teacher of Righteousness' mentioned in one of the scrolls had far more important differences than similarities with Jesus. And the similarities were simply things that were commonplace in the Jewish culture of that era.

For a good many years, it appeared that the main importance of the Dead Sea Scrolls would be to give scholars much more ancient manuscripts of certain Old Testament books, such as Isaiah, than had hitherto been available. And this was a valuable contribution because it showed that these documents had undergone very minor alterations in a thousand years of scribal copying.

But all this time, unknown to the public, a dedicated Spanish professor named Jose O'Callagahan, of the Pontifical Biblical Institute in Rome, was painstakingly trying to fit together nineteen tiny fragments of papyrus which had been found among the scrolls. In early 1972 – years after other scholars were convinced of the correctness of his thesis – he finally published in a learned journal the conclusion that these were fragments of a copy of the Gospel According to Mark. And they could be dated scientifically as having been written about A.D. 50.

The date is tremendously significant. Until this discovery was made, biblical scholars had assumed that Mark's gospel – evidently the oldest of the four contained in the New Testament – had been written in Rome between A.D. 65 and 68. The author, John Mark, is mentioned several times in the Acts of the Apostles as a young companion and assistant of Paul and later of Peter. It is clear from the text that what he set down in his Gospel is based on the first-hand personal recollections of Peter. But if the gospel had been written, as previously supposed, as late as A.D. 68, some thirty-eight years would have gone by since Jesus' death, and Peter would have been an old man. It was these assumed 'facts' that made it easy for form critics to postulate that the story of Jesus – passed along for nearly four decades by word of mouth or in now-lost documents – had acquired a heavy intermixture of myth and legend.

But if Mark's gospel were written within a dozen or so years of Jesus' death – as it must have been if a copy had circulated so far as the Essene library by A.D. 50 – then it had to survive the acid test of all historical writing or journalism: namely, being published at a time when it could be read, criticized and, if inauthentic, denounced by people who were alive and present at the time the alleged events occurred. Let me assure you, as a reporter, nothing makes a writer more careful of his facts that the knowledge that he'll be read by someone who can say, 'I was there'.

Moreover, the fact that the early Christian community chose Mark as one of only four Gospels (out of dozens in circulation) to be preserved for posterity in what we now call the 'canon' of New Testament is further evidence that the people closest to the events – Jesus' original followers – found Mark's report to be accurate and trustworthy – not myth, but true history.

The Gospels of Matthew and Luke correspond very closely to that of Mark, but contain valuable additional details which obviously came from other sources. Matthew seems to have had available a collection of Jesus' teachings and sayings – perhaps from the famous 'Q' document which scholars have long postulated but so far have not been able to find. Luke had 'Q' – or whatever it was – plus the fruits of his own extensive work. A highly educated Greek physician, he came to the Holy Land after Jesus' death, and spent at least two years patiently and carefully digging up facts. It is obvious to any writer that one of his prime sources was Jesus' mother, Mary, whose viewpoint is beautifully reflected in Luke's account of the Nativity, and again in his poignant story of the crucifixion. Personally, I regard Luke as the ablest reporter, the most careful researcher, and by far the finest writer in the New Testament, and recommend that you read his Gospel first.

The fourth Gospel, attributed to the disciple John, was for years a bone of contention, with some form critics contending it contained 'Greek' ideas and thought forms that did not enter into Christianity until about 300 years after Jesus' death. To spare you a long dissection, it will suffice to say that this is now almost universally recognized as nonsense. The fourth Gospel may have been written by a disciple of John, instead of the old gentleman himself, just as Peter's recollections were set down by young John Mark. But there is no longer any sound scholarly reason for doubting that the last Gospel originated in the first century, not too many years after the events it records, and within the probable lifetime of the Apostle whose name it bears.

There is one peculiarity about John's Gospel which is more readily obvious to a professional writer and editor than it may be to a layman, and I think I should warn you of it. John is inclined to attribute directly to Jesus, words and thoughts that almost certainly represent

John's own views of what Jesus *meant* to say, or *would* have said in a particular circumstance. Since direct quotes were not used in the Greek manuscript of the Gospels, it is hard to tell where Jesus' actual words leave off and John's interpretations of them begin. This need not cause any serious hangups for the modern reader.

The rest of the New Testament – particularly the letter of the apostle Paul to the young churches in Asia Minor, which were written beginning as early as A.D. 56, also provide valuable additional data about the life and teaching – and above all, about the *spirit* of Jesus.

The remarkable thing about all of these ancient documents is that even though written at different times and places by different men, they all present a clearly recognizable picture of the same powerful personality. There can be no question in the mind of anyone who has read the New Testament with an open mind that this is an essentially authentic account of the real life of a real person. As J. B. Phillips has well said, the Gospels have 'the ring of truth'.

CHAPTER THREE

Birth and early days

No one knows exactly when or where Jesus was born, but we can be reasonably certain the event did *not* take place – as millions today assume – in a wooden stable in Bethlehem on 25th December in the year A.D. 1.

The only aspect of that traditional version of Jesus' birthday which has any claim to historical accuracy or biblical backing is the part about Bethlehem. Both Matthew and Luke – the only two Gospels which contain nativity narratives – agree that Jesus was born at Bethlehem while his parents, Mary and Joseph, were on a brief visit to that little village in the foothills of Judea. They had made the trip from their home town of Nazareth to Bethlehem, with Mary nine months pregnant and obviously very uncomfortable riding a donkey, because the Roman Emperor Augustus had decreed that everyone in the empire must return to the place of his birth on a certain date in order to pay a head tax, one of Imperial Rome's favoured methods of raising money for its endless wars.

Joseph did his best to find comfortable lodgings for his imminently-expectant wife, but Bethlehem's only inn was already overflowing with guests. The innkeeper has been unfairly reviled over the centuries as a cold-hearted chap who turned away the mother of Jesus in her hour of need. But he actually must have been a kind man. Even though the inn itself was full, he invited Mary and Joseph to lodge in a cave under the hillside structure which was used to house cattle in cold weather. Such caves, hollowed out of the soft limestone rock of the Judean hills, are used to this day as cattle housing. The wooden cow-barn or stable, which appears in so many Renaissance paintings and which continues today to be the centrepiece of Christmas crêches, is entirely a product of Western imagination. It is *our* idea of the kind of place where cattle are kept, not Bethlehem's.

In a Bethlehem cattle-cave, trenches are hollowed out on the floor to be filled with straw for the beasts housed there. They are called 'mangers', and it was in one of these humble beds that Mary lay when she gave birth to the infant who was to make a greater impact on history than anyone else who ever lived.

We can be sure the month was not December because that careful reporter, Luke (whose birth narrative plainly is based on interviews with Mary herself), records that 'there were some shepherds in that part of the country who were spending the night in the fields, taking care of their flocks'. It is much too cold and rainy in Judea in December for shepherds and their flocks to remain outside in the fields overnight. But to this day, Judean shepherds and sheep do exactly that during the warm nights near the end of summer. So – since the Bible gives no other hint as to a date – September or early October seems the best guess as to the actual time of Jesus' birth.

As for the year, we know it was not A.D. 1 for a very

simple reason. The Roman monk Dionysius Exiguus, who was assigned by a sixth-century pope to translate the traditional Roman calendar into a new Christian calendar dating all events before (B.C.) or after (A.D.) the birth of Jesus, was a terrible mathematician. A re-check of his figures reveals that he misplaced the anchor year by at least six, perhaps seven years. There is corroborating evidence, too complex to go into here, which convinces virtually all modern scholars that the actual year of Jesus' birth was either 6 B.C. or 7 B.C.

The custom of celebrating Jesus' birth on 25th December originated in the fourth century A.D. as part of a deliberate attempt by the Church to 'Christianize' a pagan Roman festival celebrating the winter solstice, the date on which the days cease to grow shorter and begin to grow longer.

The revelry attending this festival had become quite raucous, and the Church fathers, seeing no hope of repealing such a popular party season, sought to give it religious significance by arbitrarily declaring it the date of 'Christ's Mass', the official celebration of Jesus' birth.

They were, of course, only partially successful. I find it very ironic today to see Christians wringing their hands over the revelry, gift-giving and commercialism that, they say, has 'paganized' Christmas. The truth is that Christmas is not a Christian holiday that has become partly paganized: it is, and always has been, a pagan holiday partly Christianized.

One aspect of the birth of Jesus that has caused a disproportionate amount of quarrelling among Christians is the assertion that Mary became pregnant without ever having had sex relations with her husband Joseph or any other man.

This is the so-called doctrine of the Virgin Birth. Some Christians consider it one of the 'fundamental' beliefs of Christianity, and would like to exclude from the Church anyone who doesn't subscribe to it. If they did so, among those they'd have to drive out would be the apostle Paul and the authors of two of the New Testament Gospels, who do not mention the Virgin Birth and apparently never heard of it. Indeed, they might even have to excommunicate the author of Matthew's Gospel, who, although he explicitly states that Jesus was miraculously conceived without the agency of a human father, goes on to give a genealogy which traces Jesus' bloodline back to King David *through Joseph*, which would make sense only if Matthew meant to imply that Jesus was begotten by Joseph.

The only thing less reasonable – in my opinion, and this is a subject on which everyone seems ready to fight – than making belief in the Virgin Birth a 'test of faith' is dogmatically denying that it could or did occur. To borrow a line Jesus once used in an entirely different connection, 'with man it is impossible, but with God all things are possible'.

It is simply absurd – *in my opinion* – to argue that the Author of the Universe, the Creative Spirit who invented the whole process of natural procreation, cannot set it aside and bring a human life into being by other means any time he chooses to do so.

I am personally attached to the story of the Virgin Birth, not because I regard it as an incredible miracle which certifies the unique status of Jesus, but simply because I have learned from the Bible that God seems to make frequent use of a form of communication which I have come to call 'an enacted parable' as a device for getting across to us thick-headed humans some deep truth that would elude us if cast in purely verbal or propositional terms. The story of the Virgin Birth has been for 2,000 years an enormously successful way of conveying the idea that Jesus was a unique person with divine as well as human attributes. The doctrine thus seems to me to derive its primary importance from the fact that it points towards what really is a fundamental concept of the Christian faith – the Incarnation. We'll have more to say later about the meaning of this term, Incarnation, but it will suffice here to say that it is an Anglicized Greek word meaning that the Word of God (the very essence of God's character) was embodied (incarnate) in a human being.

Of Jesus' childhood, we have little reliable information. The early Church was flooded with 'gospels' that purported to record incidents from Jesus' boyhood, but its opinion of the authenticity of these accounts is reflected in its decision *not* to include them in the canon of the New Testament.

Of the two canonical Gospels that do allude to Jesus as a child, Matthew contributes only the bare information that Jesus grew up in Joseph's home in Nazareth. Nazareth was, and still is, a small village of lower Galilee, about twenty miles inland from the Mediterranean and some fifteen miles south of the Sea of Galilee. It lies in a hill-nestled valley about 1,300 feet above sea-level, and has a moderate climate, with enough rainfall to make for good crop-growing conditions. The importance of agriculture in Nazareth's life is reflected in Jesus' teaching, which makes frequent use of metaphors or stories drawn from such pursuits as the sowing of seed, the harvesting of grain and grapes, and the tending of sheep.

But Joseph was not a farmer. We know from Luke that he was a carpenter, which tells us quite a lot about him. The carpenters of Galilean villages were important men. They were responsible not only for the building and repair of houses, but, more significantly to the life of the community, for the production of most agricultural tools and household furnishings. As a carpenter, Joseph was a highly skilled artisan who was indispensable to his community's welfare.

That Jesus went to work for Joseph in his early life as an apprentice or helper in the carpenter shop is not explicitly stated in any of the gospels, but is so logical an inference we can hardly avoid making it. That's the way things were done in Galilean households, and after telling us that Jesus was a husky boy, dutiful to his parents, Luke probably thought it unnecessary to add that Jesus like all other boys his age at that time and place, divided his day between attendance at the synagogue school and working for Joseph in the carpenter shop.

What Luke does say of Jesus' growing up is one of the most succinct and moving sentences of the whole Bible:

'And Jesus grew both in body and in wisdom, gaining favour with God and men.'

Luke adds one vignette of Jesus' youth which no other Gospel contains, and which certainly is meaningful in view of Jesus' later career. When Jesus was twelve years old, he accompanied his parents to

Jerusalem to celebrate the Feast of the Passover. It probably was the first time he was considered old enough to join the family on this annual pilgrimage dear to every devout Jew.

'When the days of the feast were over, they (Joseph and Mary) started back home, but the boy Jesus stayed in Jerusalem,' Luke reports. 'His parents did not know this; they thought he was with the group, so they travelled a while that day and then started looking for him among their relatives and friends.

'When they did not find him, they went back to Jerusalem looking for him.

'On the third day, they found him in the Temple, sitting with the Jewish teachers, listening to them and asking questions. All who heard him were amazed at his intelligent answers.'

This anecdote tells us two things about the young Jesus. First, though polite, he was a pretty bold youngster for it took nerve for a mere boy of twelve to dare join the crowd of adult students who were engaged in Socratic dialogue with the famous rabbis of the Jerusalem Temple. Second, the fact that the rabbis let him stay – and even began to draw him out on esoteric questions about the Law – is clear evidence that, even at that tender age, he had indisputable marks of genius.

Mary recognized this, and although she fussed at Jesus a bit, as mothers will when relieved after long anxiety over a child, she was secretly pleased. Luke, who got the story from her, reports that Mary, once safely home in Nazareth, reflected on her boy's brilliant showing among the Temple rabbis and 'treasured these things in her heart'.

CHAPTER FOUR

The carpenter who shut up shop

Jesus remained in Nazareth, a hard-working, popular young man, until he was about thirty-three or thirty-four years old. Under the Jewish customs of that time, a young man usually would have married long before he reached thirty, and some recent authors, not unaware of the sensation they could thereby cause, have postulated that Jesus must have been a married man. But there is not a syllable in any of the Gospels to suggest that Jesus had a wife. And his itinerant ministry, sleeping often in open fields and never knowing where the next meal was coming from, was so incompatible with marriage that Jesus may well have chosen celibacy because he had an early intimation that no wife would be happy with the kind of life he would have to lead.

In any case, Jesus' celibacy cannot be taken as an indication that he was any kind of sexual deviate (another suggestion put forward by some people). It is made clear over and over again in the Gospels – and for this, if nothing else, we are indebted to the rock opera *Jesus Christ, Superstar* – that Jesus liked women, was always kind to them, and upheld their rights in an age when most males regarded females as mere chattel. Moreover, it is obvious that women found Jesus enormously attractive, so much so that they tagged around after him and brought him 'foolish' gifts. This simply is not the picture of a sexual deviate. One of the most pronounced traits of homosexuals, psychiatrists say, is a strong tendency towards relationships of mutual scorn with women, whom they regard as rivals with unfair natural advantages.

The event that changed Jesus' lifestyle abruptly in his early thirties was the emergence of a wilderness prophet known as John the Baptist, a rather bizarre individual who dressed in camel's hair and lived on crickets and wild honey which he scrounged in the Judean wilderness. John warned people to 'turn away from your sins because the Kingdom of heaven is near'. Most people thought that he meant the end of the world was at hand and enough were frightened by this prospect to bring John a constant flow of converts, whom he purified by 'baptizing' them in the River Jordan.

'At that time, Jesus went from Galilee to the Jordan, and came to Jordan to be baptized by him.' Matthew reports in the straightforward fashion so characteristic of the Gospels (and so maddening to a modern biographer who yearns to hear about the motivations, the inner struggles, the desires and doubts that preceded the action).

But John, who had been greeting others, including the devout Pharisees, as 'sinful snakes and vipers', seems to have sensed instantly that Jesus was another kind of person altogether. Instead of rushing him into the Jordan to wash away his sins, John 'tried to make Jesus change his mind'.

'I ought to be baptized by you,' he told Jesus.

But Jesus insisted, and when he told John that it was God's will to do it this way, John put up no further argument. Jesus was baptized in the River Jordan, and as he came up out of the water, he felt himself filled with the Spirit of God and conscious that he had a special mission in life, a high destiny to fulfil.

Although theologians and biblical scholars have been arguing for centuries (and will go on arguing for many more) about when and to what degree Jesus realized who he was and what he had to do, it seems fairly clear to this layman, whose only credential is that he has read the Bible attentively, that Jesus' mission was revealed to him very gradually. He obviously knew from the start that he had a special relationship to God, whom he dared to call his Father. (And it is enormously significant that the Aramaic word he used, *Abba*, is an intimate, personal term, roughly comparable to 'Dad' or 'Pop' in modern English, and certainly a much more familiar word than a devout first-century Jew ordinarily would dream of using.)

But even though Jesus knew he had been called to do something special for God, and he was unswervably determined to do it, whatever it was, he did not at first (in my opinion) know exactly what would be required of him. He had, in short, the same 'crisis of identity' – the same desperate yearning to comprehend what he ought to do with his life – that is so familiar to college students today.

How Jesus wrestled with his crisis of identity is described in vivid metaphorical language in the fourth chapter of Matthew's Gospel. Jesus went into the desert, where he remained in seclusion for forty days and nights, wrestling with a series of temptations which all were variations of the deep, universal human tendency to try to get things done the easy way. Jesus considered – and rejected – every possible short-cut, such as using God's power to bedazzle men until they would believe him and follow him anywhere. But he finally decided that God wanted him to do it the hard way, starting out as an itinerant preacher in his native province of Galilee.

He made his headquarters at Capernaum, a busy port on the north-west shore of the Sea of Galilee that was almost a metropolis compared to tiny Nazareth. Archaeologists have uncovered at Capernaum the ruins of an impressive synagogue, two storeys high and 65 feet long, which very likely is the one in which Jesus began his career as a teacher.

Before he began to teach, however, he did what every rabbi of that era did – he gathered a little band of disciples to accompany him and serve as his most intimate students. He chose twelve altogether. None of them looked particularly promising as a student. Most of them were simple fishermen or farmers. One, Matthew, was a tax collector for the Romans, the most despised job in occupied Palestine. One of the little details which the Gospels record that tells a great deal about the force of Jesus' personality is that he simply beckoned these busy men to follow him, and they abandoned their nets or their customs tables or their ploughs, and followed him.

It should always be borne in mind that Jesus was throughout his life a devout and orthodox Jew, and up to a point he behaved exactly like any other rabbi. He taught in the Capernaum synagogue every Sabbath, and 'was praised by all,' Luke says, 'because his words had authority.' This means that Jesus from the start did not follow the safe custom, dear to pedants in his time as in ours, of quoting someone else as authority for his statements. He simply laid it on the line: *I tell you* this is the way it is. This has always been the most striking characteristic of Jesus' teaching – not that it is unique (for most of it, as he said repeatedly, was simply what God had been trying in vain to tell men through Moses and the Prophets), but that it had, and still has, a ring of authority, a self-authenticating quality, a capacity for inspiring trust in what is said simply because of who said it. 'No man ever spoke like this before,' said one of his awed listeners. Nor, I think, has any man since.

CHAPTER FIVE

The basic questions

Unlike most religious teachers of his own time and since, Jesus did not dwell on fine points of theology or esoteric issues. Nor did he take refuge in the carefully hedged obscurities which were dear to first-century rabbis, and which continue to be highly cherished by the drafters of resolutions at contemporary church conventions.

The primary objective of Jesus' teaching was to offer clear and simple answers to the two most basic questions men have always asked about their relationship with the Infinite Mystery at the heart of the universe.

These questions may be phrased in a variety of ways, but they boil down to *What can I count on about God?* and *What does God expect of me?*

Jesus answered both of them with a single word: love.

Love has been called the most abused word in the English language. Certainly it has been used in recent years with such glibness and looseness of definition that it seems to cover everything and say nothing.

We cannot begin to comprehend why Jesus' teaching had such an impact on his contemporaries, why it remains such revolutionary and exciting good news today, unless we know what *he* meant by love.

To Jesus, loving someone meant caring a great deal about his happiness and welfare. Loving, as Jesus used the word, is not the same thing as liking or lusting. Whether or not we like someone is largely a matter of whether our attitudes and personalities are congenial. An intense desire to possess someone sexually, while it is an entirely normal and in most cases a healthy human trait, may be and often is called love, but it isn't the emotion Jesus had in mind when he spoke of love. It may help a bit if we note here that the Greeks, in whose language the New Testament was written, did not have *a* word for love. They had three entirely different words. Liking was *philia*, sexual love was *eros* (whence our word, erotic), and then there was *agapé* (pronounced ah-gah-pay, with the accent on the second syllable). Agapé, the kind of love Jesus talked about, is unselfish. It values another person, not because we find that person naturally likeable or sexually attractive, but simply because he or she *needs* or *want*s or is *entitled* to be loved by us.

Now that we've got semantics cleared up (I hope), we can appreciate why the Bible speaks of Jesus as 'proclaiming good news' when he told me, directly in so many words and even more vividly in parables and metaphors, that God's attitude towards us is one of *reckless, extravagant, unreasonable love.*

Think about it a moment. God does not hate you. He loves you. He does not wish to punish you for your errant ways. He seeks only to be reconciled with you. He is not a harsh judge keeping score of your sins and grimly waiting for the day he can send you into torment to pay for them. He is a rashly generous Father who is so eager to forgive you of *anything* you've ever done wrong that he does not wait to be cajoled – he hastens to confer his forgiveness at the first indication you are prepared to accept it.

Maybe you already believed that about God. If so, you knew it because the essence of Jesus' teaching has seeped into and permeated our society to a far greater extent than many realize. For it is mainly from Jesus that we have gained this concept of God as One whose dominant characteristic, in the words of Catholic scholar Andrew M. Greeley, is 'insanely generous love'.

British theologian Erik Routley notes, correctly, that human beings have a deeply ingrained tendency to suspect that God is basically hostile towards them.

Routley thinks this is a hangover from the primitive era of religion when gods were thought to be vengeful and capricious beings who had to be appeased by every means possible. (Some versions of Christianity, it must be regretfully confessed, have helped to perpetuate this unflattering concept of God.)

But Jesus vigorously contradicted all such notions about God. He said – and it *is* good news, the best possible news – that God loves the world and *all* of its inhabitants, always has loved them, and always will love them, even when they are wilfully disobedient and wantonly sinful. It is not because we are or ever can be deserving of his love, but simply because *it is his nature* to be loving, that we can expect from God a degree of mercy and forgiveness and acceptance that transcends anything we'd dare to hope for. This is what Jesus meant when he said, '*God is love*'. It is what Paul meant when he spoke of God making the supreme revelation of his love for us 'while we were yet sinners' – that is, before we had done anything whatever to merit a loving gesture from our Creator. It is what Luther meant when he said that 'we are saved by grace (the freely-given love of God) rather than works (our own merits)'.

We are all – even the best of us in the best of our moments – rather wretched, self-centred creatures when measured against any absolute standard of perfection. Jesus' good news was that God loves us anyway.

He expressed this profound truth most memorably, I believe, in a little anecdote which Swiss theologian Emil Brunner aptly described as 'the whole Gospel in miniature'. It is known as 'The Parable of the Prodigal Son', and you will find it in the 15th chapter of Luke's Gospel, beginning at the 11th verse.

It tells about a rebellious, wayward son who defies his father's authority, demands his inheritance in advance, and leaves home to live it up in a distant city.

After he runs through all of his money, the prodigal (i.e. recklessly wasteful) son is driven by hunger to return home. He has no hope that he will be accepted again as son and heir – even this wilful young man figures that would be too much to ask. But he knows his father to be a merciful person and hopes he will forgive him at least to the extent of taking him on as a hired hand.

But the father in the parable – who represents God – does not wait for his erring son to crawl back in humiliation. When the returning son is 'yet a long way off', his father recognizes him, runs out to meet him, and flings his arms around him in a welcome-home embrace. Then the father gives orders for the preparation of food and wine for a great feast of celebration, 'because my son was lost but now he has been found!'

The point of the parable is simple and clear. Jesus was saying: God is like that father. His forgiveness is not grudgingly extended. He does not stand on his dignity. He rushes out to meet every human child who turns back (and that is all the word 'repent' means – turn back) to him. And he offers the home-coming child, not punishment or a scolding, or even a throat-clearing lecture on not being so headstrong in the future, but just a warm we're-glad-to-see-you, let's-have-a-party welcome.

That is what God's love for us is like.

So where's the catch?

The catch is that Jesus said, just as explicitly, that *God expects us to love him and to love each other with the same kind of reckless generosity of spirit.*

Once, in a dialogue with a lawyer who was trying (as lawyers do to this day) to trap him with a tricky question, Jesus was asked which of the 613 carefully-defined religious laws of first-century Judaism he regarded as most important. Jesus answered without a moment's hesitation:

'You must love the Lord your God with all your heart, with all your soul, and with all your mind. This is the greatest and most important commandment. The second most important commandment is like it: You must love your fellow-man as yourself.'

In this two-part commandment, neither part of

which can be obeyed in isolation from the other, Jesus said, is summarized all that God expects of man, and all that God had sought to teach man through the Mosaic law and the great prophets of Israel.

It sounds very simple, but it is a vastly more difficult code to obey than one with hundreds of laws (and thousands of loopholes). For Jesus did *not* say we must give God a reasonable amount of attention, by going to church on Sunday and saying our prayers occasionally. He said we must make it the *first* business, the overriding concern, of life to establish and maintain a close relationship with God. We must value that relationship so highly that we are ready to sacrifice anything and everything, including life itself, rather than allow it to be ruptured. We must bend our wills to God's will, and pray for his help in doing so, until we honestly want to do *all* that he wishes rather than just enough to get by with. If you think this is easy, you obviously haven't really tried it. It is so hard that one of the most selfless Christians who ever lived, St Francis of Assisi, found it necessary to begin his prayers with the humble petition, 'Oh Lord, help me to want to love you!

'You must love your fellow-man as yourself.' Jesus called that the second most important commandment, but he virtually equated it with the first, saying that you can't do one without the other. 'How can you love God whom you haven't seen, and despise the brother whom you do see daily?' he asked, thus forever welding the two commandments as indivisibly as two faces of a coin. To love God truly, we must love our fellow-man – not necessarily in the sense of liking him and finding him a jolly good fellow, but rather in the sense of seeking his welfare, defending his rights, and protesting any wrongs done to him with as much vigour and persistence as though we, not he, were involved.

Nor is there any convenient rule of geographic proximity or blood relationship or race or nationality by which we may limit this demand to 'love your fellow-man as yourself'. Jesus made that clear in another of his greatest teaching-stories, the Parable of the Good Samaritan.

To comprehend the force of this parable, you must know that the Jews – to whom Jesus told it – looked down on Samaritans much as many white people today look down on Negroes. Samaritans were alright in their place, but one could not expect much from them in the way of honour, courage or decent behaviour.

One day, Jesus said, a man was going from Jerusalem to Jericho – a difficult trip in those days, and one that had to be made over lonely, dangerous roads. Robbers attacked the traveller – a not uncommon occurrence – stripped him of his clothing, money and other valuables, and beat him up, leaving him half dead.

In a little while, along the road came a priest. He saw the wounded man lying there, bleeding and in pain. But either he figured it was 'None of my business' or he was afraid that the robbers might still be in the vicinity. In any case, the priest ignored the wounded man and 'walked on by, on the other side' of the road.

By and by a Levite came down the road. Now the term 'Levite' probably means little to you, but it meant a lot to the first-century Jewish audience to whom Jesus told this tale. Levites were not as high in the ecclesiastical hierarchy as priests, but they regarded themselves as a long cut above the common herd. They assisted the priests at ceremonies, took care of the money, had responsibility for the care and upkeep of the sanctuary. They were, in short, rather like the deacons, elders, trustees, vestrymen, or whatever they may be called, who serve as the lay leaders of contemporary churches. They were definitely an important part of the religious Establishment.

And how did the Levite behave when he spotted the badly-injured and perhaps dying man in the ditch where the bandits had cast him? Jesus said the Levite – a little bolder than the priest, perhaps troubled by conscience, but not troubled enough – 'went over and looked at the (wounded) man, and then walked on by, on the other side'.

Finally, along came a Samaritan – one of *those* people, you know.

'And when he saw the wounded man, his heart was filled with pity,' Jesus related. 'He went over to him, poured oil and wine (the standard antiseptic of the time) on his wounds and bandaged them. Then he put the man on his own animal and took him to an inn, where he took care of him. The next day, he took out two silver coins and gave them to the innkeeper. "Take care of him," he told the innkeeper, "and when I come back this way, I will pay you back whatever you spend on him." '

Jesus then turned to his audience of Samaritan-hating Jews and bluntly asked:

'In your opinion, which one of these three acted like a fellow-man towards the man attacked by the robbers?'

There is only one answer, and a Jewish lawyer reluctantly gave it:

'The one who was kind to him.'

That was the last time anyone dared to ask Jesus: just who is this fellow-man I am commanded to love?

The parable's point should not be mistaken. Jesus was not saying that we have an equal and unlimited obligation to every man. That idea too often leads to a sterile 'love for humanity' which remains so generalized and diffuse that it somehow never seems to yield any concrete acts of love for specific human beings.

No, Jesus' point was that our duty is to extend compassion and generous assistance to those needful persons whom we encounter along our pathway through life – whether they are friends, strangers, or even enemies. We don't have to go out and beat the bushes for them; if we keep our eyes open, we'll find our pathway strewn with them. Their need may be for money or medical assistance, as in the case of the man robbed on the road to Jericho. But it may just as well be a need for understanding, or sympathy, or companionship, or acceptance. In a highly organized modern society, where government agencies perform many of the acts of mercy hitherto left to private charity, the need of our fellow-man may be for enough generosity on our part to pay willingly the taxes necessary to support good schools and hospitals, to clean up slums and build decent homes, and to provide public assistance for those unable to work.

There is more than one way of turning a blind eye to human suffering and 'going by on the other side'. Jesus said doing that was a sin – not a minor sin, nor a 'political' sin, but a violation of the one great commandment, the commandment on which all others depend.

CHAPTER SIX

The teacher

Although Jesus taught that all necessary guidelines to decent human behaviour can be deduced from the single 'great commandment' to love God and one another, he didn't hesitate when opportunity arose to offer examples of how the law of love applies to specific situations. And many of his practical applications of the law of love run directly counter to conventional morality and our natural human instincts.

For example, consider Jesus' attitude towards the practice of passing judgement on other people – a practice which unfortunately is widespread, not only among middle-aged people shocked by new customs but also among young people who look down on 'straights'.

Jesus took the position that everyone should mind his own business, and he used some pretty strong words about it.

'Do not judge others, and God will not judge you,' he said. 'Do not condemn others, and God will not condemn you.'

Could he really mean that none of us, however righteous, has any business trying to tell other people how to conduct their lives?

Yes, that's exactly what he meant.

'Why do you look at the speck in your brother's eye,

but pay no attention to the log in your own eye?' he asked. 'How can you say to your brother, "Please, brother, let me take that speck out of your eye", yet not even see the log in your own eye? You hypocrite! Take the log out of your own eye first, and then you will be able to see and take the speck out of your brother's eye.'

In other words, since all of us are imperfect, we must learn to bear with one another's faults and concentrate on correcting our own. No teaching of Jesus is so widely ignored, even among those who claim to be his followers, as this. Lack of mutual forbearance and harsh judgementalism have poisoned many human relationships in contemporary society, including those between parents and children, between black people and white people, between people who like long hair and people who like short hair, between bigots like Alf Garnett and anti-bigots who glory in their moral superiority over Alf Garnett.

Jesus never suggested that we should be neutral or indifferent about *issues*, such as bigotry. He was always forthright in taking stands on what's right and what's wrong in human relationships. But he insisted that moral judgements be directed at deeds, or attitudes, types of behaviour – never at individuals. We can and should detest bigotry: it is the very antithesis of Christian love. But we are specifically forbidden, if we would follow the way of Jesus, to condemn any *person* by labelling him a bigot. The Christian rule of tolerance is simple and absolute: 'Do not judge others.'

Another piece of conventional morality which Jesus totally repudiated is the idea that we are entitled to get even with people who've done us wrong. Some people seem to think Jesus merely tempered this idea by urging us to be patient and put up with a reasonable amount of mistreatment before we strike back. But that's not what he actually said.

He said there is *no* limit to the amount of forgiveness we must be ready to extend before we are justified in seeking vengeance. This is a very hard teaching for many people (including the hot-tempered individual who is writing these words) to accept. It is so contrary to natural inclination – and even to our natural 'sense of justice' – that Jesus' disciples thought they surely must have misunderstood him. One of them, Peter, tried to get Jesus to settle for some reasonable limitation. Peter asked: If somebody wrongs me seven times in a row, and I forgive him each time, may I not let him have it the eighth time? But Jesus replied that 'seventy times seven' would be a more appropriate standard. And of course, he did not mean to fix 490 wrongs as the maximum number a Christian is expected to absorb. He was simply using a vivid metaphor to tell Peter that the requirement to forgive others for the wrongs they do us is unlimited.

Not only is it unlimited: it is also backed up by the sternest warning in all of Jesus' teaching. 'If you forgive others the wrongs they have done you, your Father in heaven will also forgive you. But if you do not forgive the wrongs of others, then your Father in heaven will not forgive the wrongs you have done.' To make sure we would not forget this admonition that our own claim to God's forgiveness is directly dependent on our willingness to extend the same forgiveness to others, Jesus included in the model prayer he taught his disciples the sentence:

'Forgive us the wrongs we have done, as we forgive the wrongs that others have done us.'

Many people say that 'Lord's Prayer' daily. It is a good time to pause and search your heart: Is there someone you need to forgive for something today?

The sin Jesus hated worst was spiritual pride, or what we would call today self-righteousness. We are guilty of it whenever we think we are better than someone else – whether our sense of superiority is derived from the fact that we are very strict in our morals, or from the fact that we are 'free spirits' who thumb our noses at conventional rules. Some who work hard at being libertines take a more snobbish pride in the looseness of their lifestyles than priggish Puritans take in their ostentatious abstentions. Either type of smugness was equally detestable to Jesus.

His antidote for it was humility. Humility does not mean affecting great modesty about yourself or your ability. Still less does it mean grovelling self-contempt. It simply means recognizing three facts:

1. You aren't the centre of the universe: God is. What happens to you is important to Him – but so is what happens to other people.

2. At your very best, when you're being most compassionate, forgiving and non-judgemental, you're still a long way from perfect and therefore in no position to feel proud of yourself.

3. You can't be even half-good without a lot of help from God. The help he gives us is called 'grace' and we'll have more to say later on about how it's imparted

to us. But for the present, the point is that we can't make it on our own. Whatever glimmer of goodness we may possess comes to us, not through our own efforts, but as a free gift of God. So what have we to boast about?

Our natural disposition towards self-righteousness is so great that Jesus said we should go to great ends to avoid getting caught at any good deed that might cause others to praise us and inflate our opinions of ourselves.

'Be careful not to perform your religious duties in public so that people will see what you do,' he said. 'When you give something to a needy person, do not make a big show of it – do it in such a way that even your closest friend will not know about it.'

Generosity was a major theme of Jesus' teaching. He particularly stressed two principles: our giving should be done as secretly as possible, as mentioned above, and it should be recklessly generous. Not for Jesus was the nice calculation of 'my share' or 'what we can afford to give'.

'Give to others and God will give to you,' he promised. If you are extravagant in your giving, 'you will receive a full measure, a generous helping, poured into your hands – all that you can hold. The measure you use for others is the one God will use for you.'

Here again it is necessary to explain that Jesus – who frequently used flashing metaphors and hyperbole in his teaching – was not advocating generosity as a smart investment that would be returned with interest by God. He was saying that those who give generously to others are richly rewarded – not necessarily, in fact not usually, in kind, but rather in the infinitely more valuable coin of spiritual enrichment and inward peace. To receive a gift from someone is a pleasant thing, Jesus said, but to give is a much greater source of true joy.

Except as something to be given to the needy, Jesus has a rather low opinion of wealth. Indeed, his teachings on this subject are – from the viewpoint of the conventional wisdom of his day and ours – among the most genuinely radical things he ever said.

Money, he said, is dangerous stuff. It ensnares you, and subtly supplants God as the object of your deepest devotion. 'Do not save riches for yourselves here on earth,' he counselled. 'Instead save riches for yourselves in heaven – for your heart will always be where your riches are.'

And again:

'No man can be a slave to two masters: he will hate one and love the other: he will be loyal to one and despise the other. You cannot serve both God and money.'

A rich man who ignored the hunger of a beggar at his door was the villain in one of Jesus' most memorable parables. (Read it for yourself; you'll find it in the 19th through the 26th verses of the 16th chapter of Luke's Gospel.) And on one occasion, after a conversation with a wealthy young man who was prepared to do almost anything – except give up his money – to become Jesus' disciple, Jesus said with great sadness:

'It is very hard for a rich man to enter the Kingdom of Heaven.'

Young people who accuse their parents' generation of excessive materialism are apt to cheer Jesus' statements about the pitfalls of wealth. But the generational response often is reversed when we come to Jesus' teachings about sex.

No matter how hard you twist the Gospel record, you cannot make Jesus out as an advocate of free love. He was always forgiving and compassionate towards people who had succumbed to sexual temptations, and one of the most moving anecdotes in the New Testament records how he saved a married woman who had been caught in the act of adultery. The poor woman had been condemned under a Jewish law dating back to Moses, and a group of Establishment types were dragging her out to stone her to death, as the law provided. Jesus intervened. Hoping to trap him into a direct contradiction of Mosaic law – which would have enabled them to brand him a heretic – Jesus' enemies asked whether he approved of stoning the wretched woman. He replied: 'Whichever one of you has committed no sin may throw the first stone at her.' Shamed by this response, the execution party melted away, one by one, until Jesus was left alone with the woman.

'Is there no one left to condemn you?' he asked gently.

'No one, sir.'

'Then I do not condemn you either. Go, but do not sin again.'

This little story tells us three things about Jesus. First, he was deeply compassionate towards *people*, all kinds of people. Second, his presence was so commanding, his personality so forceful, that he could halt an execution without even raising his voice. And third, although merciful towards an adultress he *did* call adultery a sin, and told the woman to cut it out.

In fact, he went beyond the Old Testament command against adultery by saying that the sin was not limited to actual acts of illicit intercourse. Even to play Casanova in your fantasies by cherishing lustful desires, he said, is to 'commit adultery in your heart'.

Jesus was not anti-sex. On the contrary, he regarded sex as a sacred thing – the sacrament of marriage, ordained by God for the dual purpose of knitting a man and wife into a unique kind of oneness and of procreating children under conditions that would give them the best chance for a stable and loving home.

It was precisely because he appreciated the importance of sex in human life that Jesus insisted it should be limited to an enduring, mutually responsible relationship. It may be argued that such a relationship can exist without a formal marriage ceremony. But most of this talk about marriage being out of date is just a new version of a line that men have been feeding gullible women for countless centuries in an attempt to have sex without responsibility. In most cases – I'd say about 999 out of every 1,000 – marriage is the logical solution for a couple who seriously intend to establish an enduring, mutually responsible relationship.

And marriage is for keeps.

Jesus bore down hard on that point. He flatly disapproved of divorce. Divorce was even easier and more commonplace in his day than it is now. All a husband had to do to get rid of his wife was give her a written statement attesting that she was now a divorced woman. Both partners were then free to marry.

Jesus outraged the lawyers of Palestine by declaring that this whole system was contrary to what God had in mind when he created male and female beings and established a strong sexual attraction between them. God's idea, Jesus said, was that a man and woman should mate for life. Marriage was meant to be an indissoluble bond, and anyone who remarries after a civil divorce is actually living in adultery with a person who is not, in God's eyes, truly his or her mate.

This is a 'hard teaching' – as some of his disciples complained to Jesus at the time. But the only thing that can be said in amelioration of it, without doing violence to Jesus' teaching, is to reiterate that he was strict about principles but lenient with human beings who had weakly violated those principles.

If you know someone who has remarried after divorce, you must not assume that this person stands condemned before Jesus. That is entirely a private matter between Jesus and the person concerned, and the best clue to Jesus' attitude is the story about his gentle treatment of the woman who was about to be stoned for adultery.

CHAPTER SEVEN

His life style

Several years ago, I wrote a Christmas column for United Press International that began with these words:

'Once there was a young man who wore sandals, a beard and long hair.

'His parents were law-abiding, middle-class folks. They provided a good home for their son, sent him to the right schools, and took him to worship services every Sabbath. They expected that someday he would take over his father's business.

'But the young man had different ideas. To the distress of his parents, he turned his back on the comfortable home they had prepared for him. He left home and dropped out of respectable society . . .'

The column brought in a deluge of outraged mail, most of it from middle-aged, middle-class Americans. They said I had depicted Jesus as a 'hippie', and indicated this was sheer blasphemy.

Before I can answer this allegation, we have to settle on a definition of that loosely-used term, 'hippie'. To some people, it connotes a person who is deep into drug use, unwashed and untidy, and contemptuous of the law.

Jesus certainly was not a hippie in that sense, and

there was not a word in my column which indicated he was.

But there are plenty of critical people of mature years who have begun to apply the opprobrious label, 'hippie', to any young man or woman whose hair styles, clothing or musical tastes they disapprove. The young person in question may be highly moral; he or she may be a far more dedicated disciple of Jesus than the self-righteous older person who is so free with his condemnation. But that won't stop a modern Pharisee from flinging around that put-down word, 'hippie'.

Let's eschew the word entirely because it has acquired such confused and controversial connotations. But we still are left with a phenomenon that has profound social and religious significance. Millions of young people in our time *have* turned their backs on the excessive materialism of contemporary society. They are creating a counter-culture with vastly different values than the one in which their upward-mobile parents struggled for 'success'. They are seeking a simpler life, a closer harmony with nature, a sense of community built upon mutual sharing and honest self-revelation, and – far from least – a personal knowledge of God.

In their quest for these things, they sometimes follow a lifestyle that shocks their elders, because they seem blithely indifferent to some of the *cultural* values of the middle-class adult world. They are not convinced that cleanliness is next to godliness, nor do they regard vagrancy as scandalous. They will share their last bit of food with a stranger who's hungry, but they refuse to worry about where their next meal's coming from.

I cannot help how many people it shocks; I am compelled to report that Jesus' lifestyle was remarkably similar.

When he emerged from his period of withdrawal into the wilderness, with his identity crisis settled, he became an itinerant teacher, going from town to town in a seemingly aimless manner, talking to anyone who'd listen about what was really important in life.

His way of life, as described in the Scriptures, precisely fits the modern police-file description of a vagrant: a man with no fixed address, and no visible source of income.

Like many young people today, he was always ready to share whatever he had, and he accepted with pleasure whatever hospitality was offered to him. He had no allowance from his family (which was appalled by his conduct and sent representatives urging him to come home and resume a respectable life in Nazareth). Sometimes he went hungry, and he often slept in the fields at night.

When his disciples fretted over the insecurity of this way of life, and the irregularity of their creature comforts, Jesus rebuked them with a wonderful insouciance:

'Do not be worried about the food and drink you need to stay alive, or about clothes for your body. After all, isn't life worth more than food? And isn't the body worth more than clothes? Look at the birds flying around: they do not plant seeds, gather a harvest and put it in barns. Your Father in Heaven takes care of them! Aren't you worth much more than birds? So do not start worrying: "Where will my food come from? Or my drink? Or my clothes?" These are the things the heathen are always concerned about. Instead, be concerned above everything else with God's Kingdom and with what he requires.'

Impractical counsel? It certainly sounds so to a middle-aged parent conditioned by years of responsibility for providing for the needs of a family. But Jesus not only said those words: he *lived* that kind of life. And his refusal to worry about such relatively unimportant things as material possessions is a sharp and extremely relevant challenge to an age in which men are literally killing themselves with work and worry in the name of achieving 'security'.

Jesus beat modern psychiatry by 2,000 years to the discovery that worry – anxiety about the future – is a source of crippling stress, as well as the most futile exercise in which a person can engage.

'Which one of you can live a few more years by worrying about it?' he demanded of his worry-wart disciples. 'Do not worry about tomorrow; it will have enough worries of its own. There is no need to add to the troubles each day brings.'

'Taming' the words of Jesus through interpretation and commentary has always seemed to me a most dangerous activity for preachers, writers or theologians to undertake. It is true that Jesus' style of teaching made heavy use of hyperbole – deliberate exaggeration for effect. He deliberately overstated things in order to shock his listeners into opening their minds a tiny crack. As a realist – which he certainly was – Jesus knew that most men must work to earn a living for themselves and their family, and he did not mean to scorn their honest toil or demean the nobility of the motives of one who carries a daily burden of drudgery in order to provide food, clothing, housing, medical care and education for his children. But in acknowledging the truth of all these considerations, we must not lose the force of the words and example by which he sought to teach us that there's more to life than a home in the suburbs, balanced meals and a comfortable bank balance.

Seek God *first* and do what he requires of you – even if you have to go hungry and naked, Jesus said. And he meant exactly that. Some of history's greatest saints have come from the ranks of those, such as Francis of Assisi, who took his advice literally.

Another aspect of Jesus' lifestyle which shocked his respectable contemporaries – and which has a strong affinity with the mores of today's youth culture – is that he wasn't very choosy about the company he kept. He practised the non-judgemental tolerance which he preached, and consorted freely with people who were regarded as sinners. One of his friends was a thief, another an ex-prostitute. When more conservative religious leaders took him to task for being so careless in his choice of companions, Jesus replied that God had sent him to call sinners to repentance, not to feed the complacency of the righteous.

Although he was even prepared to go hungry when necessary to be faithful to his mission, Jesus was not an ascetic. He loved good food and good wine, and thoroughly enjoyed a good party. He was sparkling company, and much sought-after as a guest. Once, he was attending a wedding party in a town called Cana. The host ran out of wine, which was embarrassing to him as well as disappointing to the celebrants. Jesus had some earthen jugs filled with plain water, and when it was served to the guests, it had turned into fine wine. Whether one reads this anecdote of the wedding in Cana as an allegory, as some scholars do, or as literal history, it would not have been preserved in the New Testament had it been out of character for Jesus to accept the role of emergency wine-maker for an embarrassed host. It forever belies any image of Jesus as a blue-nose ascetic.

Another libel that has gained wide currency over the centuries is that Jesus was 'meek and mild' – a mousy little man who patted children on the head and never raised his voice.

Actually, we know from the Scriptures that he was a rather big man – tall enough to be readily spotted in a large crowd – with strong muscles developed by years of hard physical labour in a carpenter shop. Far from being meek and mild, he was so outspoken that he was forever trampling on the toes of the Establishment. And he was capable of getting very angry when he saw something he regarded as an outrage. Once, he entered the Temple of Jerusalem and found its courtyard filled with money-changers, pigeon salesmen and others who made a lucrative racket of defrauding pilgrims come from distant places to worship at the Temple. Jesus seized a whip, and drove the crooked merchants from the Temple courtyard, overturning their tables and smashing their stools. As they fled from his wrath, he shouted after them: 'God said, "My house will be called a house of prayer." But you are making it a hideout for thieves.'

Although he resorted to physical violence in this instance, Jesus generally had a low opinion of it. He warned that 'those who live by the sword shall die by the sword' – a statement abundantly proved by the long cruel history of human warfare. He urged his disciples to 'turn the other cheek' – to accept rebuffs, wrongs and insults without seeking to even the score with some act of revenge. But this was not the cowardly counsel of a meek man afraid of making trouble: it was a courageous man's admonition that strong people must take the initiative in breaking the petty cycle of revenge and counter-revenge that so bemuses the weak.

Jesus was soft-spoken and gentle in his dealings with timid and lowly people. But he could also be caustic. In speaking to self-righteous people, he pulled no punches in telling them what he thought of them. He was particularly severe with the religious leaders of the Palestinian Establishment – the Pharisees, Sadducees and experts on Mosaic Law – who attached great importance to the minutiae of ritual observance, but displayed no real love or compassion for their fellow men.

'You hypocrites!' he shouted at a group of prominent religious teachers in Jerusalem. 'You take advantage of widows and rob them of their homes, and then make a show of saying long prayers . . .

'Blind fools! You give to God one tenth even of the seasoning herbs you use, but you neglect to obey the really important teachings of the Law, such as justice and mercy and honesty . . . You are like whitewashed tombs, which look fine on the outside, but are full of dead men's bones and rotten stuff on the inside. On the outside you appear to everybody as good, but inside you are full of hypocrisy and sins.'

Remember that he was saying all this to their faces – casting it right into their teeth. Meek and mild? Hardly. He was a stormy, passionate, totally dedicated man, and when the authorities charged him with 'stirring up the people' – as they eventually did – it was an entirely accurate charge. The wonderful thing is that he's still stirring up people, 2,000 years later.

But Jesus was not always storming or admonishing or pleading. He was not even always earnest. On the contrary, he had a puckish sense of humour, and liked to kid his friends by giving them humorous nicknames. A lot of Jesus' wit has been lost in translation from his own tongue, Aramaic, through Greek, and finally into English. But we can still see flashes of it, as when he poked a little fun at two of his disciples who wanted to 'call down fire from Heaven' to consume hecklers who were giving them a bad time. Jesus' only response to this suggestion was to nickname the disciples 'the sons of thunder'. Similarly, he needled the notoriously wishy-washy disciple Peter by nicknaming him 'The Rock'. Often Jesus' wit comes through in the incandescent metaphors he used, such as his reference to nit-picking religionists as people who would strain a gnat out of their soup but swallow a camel without noticing it.

Although Jesus had no use for *pro-forma* religious rites, it would be a grave error to think of him as an activist who had no time for 'religion'. The truth is just the opposite. If by religion we mean prayer and Bible reading and public worship, then Jesus was a faithful practitioner of it. Indeed, faithful religious observance was the keystone of his lifestyle.

He often withdrew into isolated places – indoors, in the privacy of a closed room, or out-doors, in the gardens on the Mount of Olives – to pray. His prayers were simple, forthright conversations with his Father in Heaven, as we know from the few samples preserved for us in the New Testament, including the one we call 'The Lord's Prayer'. Jesus felt that prayer was an intensely private and personal experience, and we may deduce that he spent more time listening than talking when he communed in prayer with his Father. Certainly he had a strong sense of effective two-way communication.

'One of the truly amazing things about Jesus is the reality and directness of his own experience of God', says theologian Edward W. Bauman. When Jesus spoke of God, it was never as an 'object of thought or worship' but always as one who was 'consciously present in every moment' of Jesus' life. Jesus spoke about God with authority because he felt that he knew with absolute certainty what God is like and what God required of men.

But his incredibly open channel of communication with God did not make him scornful of the perhaps less-perfect revelations that had come to other men in the past. Jesus revered the Jewish Scriptures, and it is obvious that he spent a great deal of time reading them because he could quote them at length and enjoyed debating their obscure points with the most learned rabbis of his day. At the same time, he did not hesitate to take issue with the Scriptures – even the teachings of the revered Moses – whenever he felt they were being understood in a way contrary to the actual intent of God.

The Gospels indicate that Jesus was regular in his attendance at public worship, showing up at the synagogue every Sabbath. And those who would advocate a 'religionless Christianity' stripped of ritual practice and centred solely upon social activism should remember that Jesus himself hallowed the two principal rites of Christianity – Baptism, by submitting himself to it; and the Lord's Supper, by instituting it on the night he was betrayed and telling his disciples to continue it perpetually as a memorial to him.

It is true that the churches which bear his name have at times strayed very far from the spirit of Jesus, especially his emphasis on loving one another. One can understand why some young members of the 'Jesus movement' feel stifled in conventional churches, and sense a need to form fellowships of their own outside the existing boundaries of institutional religion. But no community can exist without some kind of structure, and a structured community is an institution in embryo. So much time and effort and money has gone into erecting the institutions we already have, it might make more sense for real disciples of Jesus to work within those institutions, reviving and reforming them, than to waste their energy on starting new ones.

CHAPTER EIGHT

The miracle worker

The Gospels report that Jesus was able to do many things men ordinarily cannot do. He healed blindness with a touch, leprosy with a word. He could restore a madman to sanity in a single brief conversation. In his hands, five barley loaves and two small fishes multiplied to become a picnic banquet for 5,000 hungry people. At his command, water became wine, a fig tree shrivelled, a raging storm was stilled. He walked on water.

What are we children of a scientific age to make of these miracle stories? Some modern biblical scholars, following the lead of German theologian Rudolph Bultmann, would simply dismiss them as legendary accretions to the authentic story of Jesus.

Reflecting a viewpoint which is extremely widespread in contemporary culture, they assume that any miracle story *must* be false, because 'miracles don't happen'. They believe this to be a 'scientific' attitude. But of course it is not. Science tells us, through observation and measurement, how nature *normally* works. But it does not and cannot rule out, *a priori*, the possibility that the Author of the system may occasionally see fit to introduce an additional cause into a natural process, and thereby achieve a different effect than usual. The additional cause in a genuine miracle is simply the will of God that it happen.

The late C. S. Lewis, the most persuasive advocate of orthodox Christianity in our century, felt it was bootless for Christians who believe in miracles to offer arguments, personal testimony or any other kind of evidence to non-believers.

Not even direct personal experience, Lewis said, can convince a man who has made up his mind in advance that miracles cannot occur.

'Whatever experiences we may have, we shall not regard them as miraculous if we already hold a philosophy which excludes the supernatural', Lewis said in a sermon preached in a London church in 1942. 'Any event which is claimed as a miracle is, in the last resort, an experience received from the senses; and the senses are not infallible. We can always say we have been the victims of an illusion. If we disbelieve in the supernatural, that is what we always shall say.

'If the end of the world appeared in all the literal trappings of the apocalyptic vision of the Book of Revelation, if the modern materialist saw with his own eyes the heavens rolled up and the great white throne appearing, if he had the sensation of himself being hurled into the Lake of Fire, he would continue forever, in that lake itself, to regard his experience as an illusion, and to find the explanation of it in psychoanalysis or cerebral pathology.'

In his recent book, *A Rumour of Angels*, sociologist Peter Berger notes that modern man is keenly conscious of the degree to which the views of people in other ages were coloured by the 'culture conditioning' of their day.

But it never seems to occur to us that *our* attitudes are equally conditioned, or warped, by the prevailing assumptions of culture in which *we* live.

Since I've never doubted that God can do anything he wants to do, my own problem with the miracles attributed to Jesus is not *whether* they occurred, but *why* they occurred.

Jesus had a horror of attracting people to him by 'signs and wonders'. He wanted to rescue people from meaninglessness and point them towards God – not to play magician. The biblical story of his temptation in the desert demonstrates that one of the first temptations he wrestled with and rejected was to become a success the easy way by putting on flashy performances as a miracle-worker.

Over and over again in the Gospels, we find him pleading with beneficiaries of his healing power to 'tell no man' what he had done for them. He went out of his way to avoid publicity for that aspect of his ministry. When his own disciples asked for 'signs' – i.e. spectacular happenings to demonstrate Jesus' power over nature – he bitterly rebuked them.

Yet, despite his strong preference to the contrary, he *did* become widely known and celebrated as a miracle worker, and many in the crowds he attracted came not to hear him teach but in hope of seeing him perform some 'wonder'.

After years of struggling with this seeming contradiction, I have come to the conclusion there were two reasons why Jesus occasionally employed his extraordinary powers in spite of his distaste for the kind of attention they inevitably attracted.

The first reason is that Jesus was such a compassionate person he simply could not restrain the impulse to reach out and help people he encountered who were sick, crippled, hungry or miserable. This is the only 'temptation' to which Jesus ever succumbed – the temptation to be merciful to people whose plight touched his heart so strongly he could not worry about the unwanted publicity that would surely attend their healing.

The second reason why Jesus performed miracles, in my opinion, is that he shared the conviction of many young people today that deeds are more eloquent than words. Many of his miracles, as recorded in the Gospels, appear to have been enacted parables, whose purpose was not to impress but to teach.

Repeatedly, we find Jesus using a healing episode as a sort of object lesson. His stilling of a storm and walking on water were intended to teach his disciples the power of faith. When he healed ten lepers, and only one returned to say thank you, he used the occasion to point out man's almost unlimited capacity for ingratitude. He healed a crippled man on the Sabbath to make the point that the Pharisaical rules of Sabbath-keeping were perverting God's intent that this holy day of rest be a boon, not a burden, to men.

There is a brief anecdote in the Gospels which seems to indicate that Jesus on one occasion used his power over nature in a rather whimsical fashion. Mark tells the story in these words:

'As they were coming back from Bethany, Jesus was hungry. He saw in the distance a fig tree covered with leaves, so he went to it to see if he could find any figs on it; but when he came to it he found only leaves, because it was not the right time for figs. Jesus said to the fig tree: No one shall ever eat figs from you again . . . Early next morning, as they walked along the road, they saw the fig tree. It was dead all the way down to its roots.'

I love this little story because it makes Jesus seem so human – and demonstrates that he had a sense of humour. He must have guessed that his disciples would be astounded by the sight of the shrivelled fig tree, and he was right. Their astonishment plainly shows through the story they preserved in the Bible.

One thing you cannot find in the Gospels is a single instance in which Jesus performed a miracle for his own selfish benefit, or in which he derived any personal gain from a miracle. Consider again the matter of the fig tree: he could just as easily have commanded it to bring forth hundreds of plump ripe figs to satisfy his hunger. But he elected to let his stomach go on growling rather than use his power over nature in that way.

CHAPTER NINE

Opposition

The authors of the Gospels were, as previously noted, relatively uninterested in the kind of chronological detail that seems so necessary to the modern news reporter. So we cannot be sure how long Jesus continued his itinerant ministry as teacher, preacher, healer of the sick and friend of the poor. It may have lasted as long as three years, or as little as one year. In any case, it was a relatively brief public career. And we do know from the Gospels that most of it was spent in the rural province of Galilee, particularly in the area surrounding the seaport of Capernaum.

The time finally came, however, when Jesus decided he must go to the capital city of Jerusalem for a face-to-face confrontation with the lawyers and religious leaders of the Palestinian Establishment whom he had so warmly denounced as hypocrites and fools.

He foresaw the outcome of this showdown with Authority, and plainly warned his disciples, before leaving Galilee, that the visit to Jerusalem would be, for him, a one-way trip.

His forebodings upset the disciples, who were not conspicuous, at that stage, for their courage. 'They were now on the road going up to Jerusalem,' Mark reports.

'Jesus was going ahead of his disciples, who were filled with alarm.'

It was on the road to Jerusalem that two of the disciples, James and John, who were particularly close friends of Jesus, came to him with the request that they be given seats of honour, on his right hand and his left hand, when he ascended his throne. In spite of all he had tried to teach them, they were still thinking of him as Messiah in the traditional Jewish sense of an earthly-king! The other ten disciples heard of this sneaky effort by James and John to win special preference, and became angry about it. Jesus must have been pretty discouraged by this outbreak of rampant self-seeking in his innermost circle of friends. But always, he seized the 'teachable moment'.

'He called them all together', Mark says, and told them:

'You know that the men who are considered rulers of the people have power over them, and the leaders rule over them. This, however, is not the way it is among you. If one of you wants to be great, he must be the servant of the rest; and if one of you wants to be first, he must be the slave of all.'

This concept – that it is better to serve than to be served – has great appeal to many young people today. Few of them realize that it originated with Jesus 2,000 years ago.

Jesus was by this time quite a celebrity in the provinces of Palestine. When he approached the ancient city of Jericho, a huge crowd of curious people lined the streets to get a glimpse of this itinerant rabbi who was supposed to be able to heal the sick. One member of the crowd was a blind beggar named Bartimaeus. Shunted back by the crowd, bewildered and confused by all the noise, Bartimaeus called out piteously, 'Have mercy on me!' Somehow, Jesus heard that plaintive cry over the tumult. He stopped short and insisted that the blind beggar be brought to him. 'What do you want me to do for you?' Jesus asked. 'Teacher, I want to see again,' said Bartimaeus. 'Go,' Jesus said. 'Your faith has made you well.' And, Mark reports, Bartimaeus' sight was instantly restored.

When Jesus and his party arrived in Bethphage, a suburb of Jerusalem, Jesus sent two of his disciples on into the city with instructions to borrow a donkey. He had decided to make his fateful entry into Jerusalem riding on a donkey's back – a highly symbolic act to Jews who recalled what the prophet Zechariah had said of the Coming of the Messiah:

'Shout aloud, O people of Jerusalem,

'Lo, your king comes to you . . . humble and riding on an ass.'

The people – thousands of them – did shout aloud. They shouted the words of greeting so long reserved for the Messiah: 'God bless him who comes in the name of the Lord. God bless the kingdom . . .' In their enthusiasm, they stripped branches from palm trees and spread them on the road – the sign of royal welcome.

All of this popular acclaim was duly reported to the Establishment, and deepened its conviction that this fellow Jesus was a dangerous agitator who would have to be put down soon.

If any doubt remained in the minds of the chief priests that Jesus had to go, it was removed the next day when Jesus went to the Temple of Jerusalem – most sacred spot on earth to every devout Jew – and broke up the temple rackets in which the chief priests had a highly profitable personal interest.

Mark reports:

'The chief priests and the teachers of the Law heard of this, so they began looking for some way to kill Jesus.'

But they were afraid to arrest him at the Temple, because he was constantly surrounded by people who looked upon him as a hero and perhaps as the long-awaited Messiah.

For a week, Jesus made life miserable for the ruling class in Jerusalem. By day, he taught and healed the sick at the Temple, drawing ever-larger crowds. At night, he slipped quietly out of town to sleep in the home of friends at suburban Bethany. Unable to catch him alone to arrest him, the chief priests and their zealous allies in orthodoxy, the Pharisees, sought to make a fool of Jesus by trapping him with loaded questions in front of the crowds that gathered to hear him teach at the Temple. On one occasion, for example, they asked him: 'Is it against our (Jewish) law for us to pay taxes to the Roman Emperor, or not?' It was a very tricky question. If Jesus approved the payment of taxes to the Emperor, he would alienate many of the common people who heartily detested the Roman army of occupation in their country. But if Jesus said Jews should not pay taxes to Rome, the chief priests could turn him over to Roman authorities as a teacher of subversive political doctrine.

'Jesus saw through their trick', Luke records. He

asked the questioners to show him one of the coins which were the legal currency of Palestine.

'Whose face and name are on this money?' Jesus asked.

'The Roman Emperor's,' they replied.

'Well, then,' said Jesus, 'pay to the Emperor what belongs to him, and pay to God what belongs to God.'

After coming out on the losing end of several such encounters, the priests and Pharisees gave up on the attempt to entrap Jesus with his own words. But they did not waver in their determination to put him to death as soon as they could manage it without stirring up a riot among the common people who 'continued to hear Jesus gladly'.

Jesus' enormous popularity with the rank and file of the Jewish people cannot be too strongly emphasized, for it is the complete answer to any prejudiced Christian who speaks of 'the Jews' as the killers of Jesus. It was *not* 'the Jews' but a very small minority of the ruling class who had Jesus put to death – and they had to wait quite a while to bring off their dark deed because, as the Gospels say over and over again, 'they were afraid of the reaction of the people'.

Finally, as the time approached for the great Jewish festival of the Passover, the chief priests got their break. One of Jesus' disciples, Judas Iscariot, went to the chief priests with an offer to show them where they could arrest Jesus at night, with no crowds around. We can only speculate why Judas chose to betray his master. The most popular guess among biblical scholars is that Judas was a zealot who had expected Jesus to lead a political revolution against Roman rule. When he discovered Jesus really *meant* that his Kingdom was 'not of this world', Judas became disillusioned and sold him out.

Judas' price was 'thirty pieces of silver', which may not sound like a lot of money but actually represented, at that time, the equivalent of four months' wages for an ordinary labourer. So perhaps we cannot rule out the possibility that it was not political zealousness, but simple greed, that motivated Judas to become the arch-traitor of history.

CHAPTER TEN

Arrested

A typical house in first-century Jerusalem was built around a central courtyard, or atrium. All ground floor rooms opened off this courtyard. The better class of home also had a second-storey room, reached by an outside stairway. This upper room was usually quite large and was used to house guests, or for banquests.

On his fifth night in Jerusalem, Jesus had supper with his disciples in the upper room of a house in Jerusalem. The room had been placed at Jesus' disposal by a man whose name has been lost to history, but who we may presume to have been both hospitable and wealthy. Ancient Jewish custom prescribed that a teacher have a fellowship meal with his disciples on the eve of a great religious festival such as the Passover.

This meal was not the same as the Seder, the ritual feast which opens the Passover celebration. It was a much more informal, intimate kind of affair, held twenty-four hours before the sundown which signalled the beginning of Passover. Unlike the Seder menu, which has many courses, prescribed in minute detail in Mosaic law, the fellowship supper consisted only of bread and wine. The wine was drunk from a common cup, passed around the table from one person to the next.

When the hour arrived for the meal to begin – that would have been at sundown – Jesus took his place at the centre of the long table, around which his disciples had gathered. After giving thanks, he picked up a loaf of bread and broke it into fragments, which he distributed among the disciples. 'Take and eat it', he said. 'This is my body.' Then he lifted the common cup, gave thanks to God, and passed the wine among the disciples with the admonition: 'Drink it, all of you, for this is my blood, which seals God's covenant, my blood poured out for many for the forgiveness of sins.'

The disciples didn't know quite what to make of these solemn pronouncements. And they certainly had no inkling that they were participating in the first observance of what would become the central rite of the Christian religion.

Before they had time to question Jesus about his strange statements about the bread being his body and the wine his blood, the disciples were thrown into shock by another remark by Jesus.

'I tell you the truth', he said sadly. 'One of you is going to betray me.'

The disciples looked around at each other, wondering who the traitor was, and each anxious to convey his own surprised innocence. Finally, outspoken Simon Peter asked bluntly, 'Who is it , Lord?' Jesus indicated Judas. He spoke to Judas quietly, without rancour: Get on with what you've promised to do. Judas must have been surprised to find that Jesus knew of his betrayal. But he went ahead with it anyway. He hurried out of the upper room to keep his rendezvous with the chief priests, who had assembled their henchmen to seize

Jesus as soon as Judas told them where he could be found.

Jesus could have upset the whole conspiracy simply by deviating from his usual custom of going out after supper to a garden called Gethsemane, on the sloping side of the Mount of Olives. This was his favourite place in Jerusalem, the place he went to pray and meditate.

On this particular evening, he took his three closest friends among the disciples – Peter, James and John – to a secluded part of the garden, somewhat apart from the place where the other disciples were saying their evening prayers. 'Grief and anguish came over him,' Matthew reports. Jesus confided to his three friends that 'the sorrow in my heart is so great it almost crushes me.' Then he threw himself face down on the ground and the awe-stricken disciples heard him cry aloud to God:

'My Father, if it is possible, take this cup away from me! But not what I want, but what you want.'

In their eagerness to protect the doctrine of Jesus' divinity, some Christians tend to play down his humanity. But this is not piety: it is heresy, and has been so labelled by the church since its beginnings. The Bible plainly teaches that, whatever else he may have been, Jesus was fully and completely human. I stress this fact here because you cannot grasp the real poignancy of Jesus' anguish in the Garden of Gethsemane unless you bear firmly in mind that he had a normal human dread of suffering and death. He knew what lay ahead of him – and he wished with all his heart that he might be spared from it. But even in this dark hour, when his normal insouciance broke down and gave way to deep, racking fear, Jesus remained absolutely subservient to the will of God. 'Not what I want, but what you want.' He was, in Paul's great phrase, 'obedient even unto death'.

Judas knew where to find Jesus, and he led a band of soldiers and Temple guards directly to Jesus' place of prayer in the garden. They were armed with swords, and carried lanterns and torches. But they need not have feared that Jesus would run away. He walked out to meet them.

'Who are you looking for?' he asked.

'Jesus of Nazareth.'

'I am he.'

The terrified disciples expected to be arrested too, but Jesus told the soldiers, 'Since I am the one you want, let these others go.' And the soldiers, recognizing the voice of command even in a prisoner, promptly did as he said.

They tied up Jesus and led him away to the palace of the High Priest. 'The High Priest questioned Jesus about his disciples and about his teaching,' John relates. Jesus answered: 'I have always spoken publicly to everyone; all my teaching was done in the synagogues and in the Temple, where all the Jews come together. I have never said anything in secret. Why, then, do you question me? Question the people who heard me. Ask them what I told them – they know what I said.'

One of the guards considered this an impertinent answer. He slapped Jesus in the face – the first of many such blows Jesus was to receive that long night.

'Then,' says Matthew, 'the chief priests and the whole Council tried to find some false evidence against

Jesus, to put him to death, but they could not find any, even though many came up and told lies about him.'

Finally, the High Priest directly challenged Jesus:

'In the name of the living God, I now put you on oath: tell us if you are the Messiah, the Son of God.'

Jesus would not claim the title of Messiah – which he had always disliked because of its connotations of earthly kingship. But he minced no words in claiming a special relationship with God. Referring to himself simply as 'The Son of Man' – the one title he ever claimed – he told the High Priest:

'You will see the Son of Man sitting at the right side of the Almighty.'

To a devout Jew well versed in Old Testament prophecies about the Messiah, this statement was a clear-cut assertion by Jesus that he was indeed the 'anointed one', a special messenger from God, so long awaited by Israel.

'Blasphemy!' cried the High Priest. 'We don't need any more witnesses. Right here you have heard his wicked words. What do you think?'

The Council (the Jews called it the Sanhedrin, and it was the ruling body of Judaism) quickly returned its foreordained verdict:

'He is guilty, and must die.'

Then they gathered around him and spat in his face and cuffed him to show their contempt for his 'blasphemous' claim.

It was the policy of Imperial Rome to grant considerable autonomy to local ruling councils, such as the Sanhedrin, in the enforcement of religious laws and customs in occupied countries like Palestine. But there was one strict limitation on the Sanhedrin's powers. It could not impose the death penalty on anyone. That power was reserved to the Roman governor.

The governor in Jerusalem at this time was an ambitious, wishy-washy fellow named Pontius Pilate. He was eager to oblige the Jewish leaders, because he wanted to keep them tractable and avoid any threat of insurrection which would have been severely frowned upon in Rome. Therefore, Pilate was ready to listen sympathetically when the high priests brought Jesus before him, in chains. The high priests knew that a charge of blasphemy would carry no weight with Pilate, so they accused Jesus of being a subversive. Specifically, they said, he was stirring up revolution by proclaiming himself 'King of the Jews'. This put the whole case on a political basis – Jesus was depicted as a threat to Roman rule.

'Are you King of the Jews?' Pilate asked the weary figure in chains.

'Does this question come from you, or have others told you about me?' Jesus replied.

'It was your own people and their chief priests who handed you over to me,' Pilate said. 'What have you done?'

'My kingdom does not belong to this world,' Jesus said. 'I was born and came into the world for one purpose – to speak the truth.'

'And what is the truth?' Pilate asked with that casual cynicism so much in vogue in Rome's ruling circles at the time.

But Pilate was basically an honest man – even though a coward. He went back to the high priests and told them he could find no reason to condemn Jesus to death.

'I will have him whipped and let him go,' Pilate said.

But the high priests had collected a rabble of layabouts and drunks from the streets and taverns, and on signal this noisy mob began to shout demands that Jesus be put to death.

Pilate tried to pacify the crowd, but they drowned him out with cries: 'To the cross with him! To the cross!'

'But what crime has he committed?' Pilate asked.

But, Luke records, the crowd went on shouting at the top of their voices that Jesus should be crucified, so Pilate gave in and passed the death sentence they demanded. First, however, he went through what surely must be the most meaningless little ritual in human history. He called for a bowl of water, and washed his hands, a gesture intended to indicate that he personally accepted no responsibility for shedding innocent blood.

CHAPTER ELEVEN

Executed

As soon as Pilate's little hand-washing charade was completed, Roman soldiers seized Jesus roughly and hustled him off to their barracks.

Long years of occupation duty in Palestine had filled these soldiers with a deep hatred for the proud people whom they kept in subjugation, and they welcomed the chance to vent their anti-Semitism on one who was called 'The King of the Jews'.

They bound him by the wrists to a post and took turns lashing his bare back with a whip made of leather straps weighted with metal. Such a scourging often resulted in death, but the legionnaires were careful this time to stop while the prisoner was still semi-conscious.

Then they had a little fun with him. They draped a scarlet legionnaire's cloak around his bleeding shoulders, in imitation of a royal purple robe, and thrust a crown of plaited thorns on his head. One by one they approached, kneeling before him in mock homage, arising to spit in his face.

About 8 a.m. they led him out to crucify him.

When they arrived at the hill outside Jerusalem that was used for executions, they stripped the prisoner naked, and divided his clothing among them.

They set him astride a wooden peg which jutted out from the upright pole of the cross, stretched his arms wide along the crossbeam, and drove nails through the palms of his hands to hold him in place. His feet were nailed, one over the other, to the upright pole.

Crucifixion was the most agonizing death that Rome had been able to devise, and was reserved for dangerous people suspected of fomenting revolutions.

A crucified man died a lingering death, not from loss of blood but from the cumulative shock of excruciating pain. The Roman author Cicero records that many of the victims became raving madmen, and it was sometimes necessary to cut out their tongues to put a stop to their terrible screams and curses.

But this was a most unusual prisoner. As he looked down from the cross at the people who were laughing and sneering at his plight, he was heard to say:

'Father, forgive them, for they know not what they do.'

He hung there for six hours before he died.

Even in his final hour, he did not become preoccupied with his own suffering. He was still concerned for others. He saw his mother weeping at the foot of the cross, and asked a friend to take her under his care.

But even Jesus could not remain entirely serene under the prolonged physical agony of crucifixion. At one point, he cried out in despair:

'My God, my God, why have you forsaken me?'

Biblical scholars are fond of pointing out that these are the opening words of the 22nd Psalm, which concludes with a triumphant reaffirmation of faith in God.

They suggest that Jesus was merely trying to recite the Psalm.

But I think this rather glib explanation fails to do justice to the extent of Jesus' suffering on the cross. In the moment that he uttered that cry, accusing God of forsaking him, Jesus drank the cup of humanity to its dregs. For it was then that he was deprived, at least briefly, of the one support – his incredibly direct and immediate awareness of God's presence – that might have made his ordeal less awful than it would have been for an ordinary man.

As the end neared, the sun, which hitherto had been shining brightly, disappeared behind high clouds and an eerie darkness covered the whole countryside. This detail is recorded in three of the four Gospels, which indicates it made a great impression on the eyewitnesses of the crucifixion.

Exhausted by pain, Jesus slumped on the cross and cried out in a loud voice:

'Father, in your hands I place my spirit.'

It was finished. A moment later, he died.

The Roman officer who had supervised the execution had been puzzled throughout by the strange conduct of this gentle and courageous young Jew. Now, deeply moved, he gravely saluted the corpse on the cross and said:

'He was a good man.'

CHAPTER TWELVE

'A mighty act!'

Jesus was crucified on a Friday. His body was placed in a tomb, which was sealed with a large stone. The burial was completed just before sundown, the hour at which the Sabbath officially began.

The Jewish laws of Sabbath observance strictly forbade any kind of manual labour, including preparation of a corpse for entombment. So the job of anointing Jesus' body with embalming spices – customarily performed by female relatives – had to wait until the Sabbath was over.

Early Sunday morning, while it was still dark, three women who had been followers of Jesus set out for the tomb to embalm his body. They arrived just at sunrise.

The stone had been rolled away from the entrance. The tomb was empty.

That is the story the New Testament Gospels tell. If you find it hard to believe, so did the people who first heard it. When the terrified women ran back to the house in Jerusalem, where many of Jesus' male disciples were in hiding, their report was at first dismissed as nonsense.

In our time, some distinguished Christian theologians have viewed the story of the empty tomb as a mythological projection of the disciples' belief that Jesus had triumphed over death. According to this view, Jesus' body remained in the tomb and eventually rotted away like all other human bodies. When the disciples proclaimed his return from death, they meant only that he had come to life again in their minds and hearts.

This 'demythologized' interpretation has great appeal for all who find themselves unable to accept the possibility that God might intervene in the operation of nature to raise a dead man to life.

But however congenial it may be to the mind-set of our age, the concept of a purely spiritual resurrection is difficult to square with the historical facts as we know them, not only from the New Testament but from other sources.

It is clearly established history that within a short time after Jesus' crucifixion, his disciples began to proclaim that he had risen from the grave. And they made the claim publicly in Jerusalem.

It was obviously in the interests of the Jewish and Roman authorities to spike this story. And they could have done so, quickly and conclusively, simply by showing that Jesus' body was still in the tomb. Their failure to employ this perfect refutation strongly suggests that they were unable to produce the body.

Of course, an empty tomb does not by itself mean that its occupant has returned to life. The body could have been secretly removed by Jesus' followers to give credence to their preaching of a resurrection.

What's wrong with the stolen-body theory? Its basic fallacy is that it would mean that Jesus' followers were telling a deliberate lie when they said he had been raised from death by an act of God. And any such idea contradicts all that we know about human nature.

As New Testament historian Daniel P. Fuller has pointed out, the disciples 'preached the risen Jesus at the risk of their lives' and 'men do not risk their lives for what they know to be a fraud'.

Another explanation is that Jesus did not really die on the cross, but merely went into a deathlike coma, either from shock or from drinking wine spiked with a drug.

This explanation raises far more questions than it answers. For example: were Roman legionnaires so naïve as to hand over a condemned criminal to his friends without first making sure he was dead?

The Gospels record that they did make sure. Even though Jesus appeared to be already dead, they plunged a spear deep into his side to snuff out any possible spark of life.

Suppose that Jesus had revived in the tomb. He would have been in critical condition from six hours of torture on the cross and loss of blood from the spear wound. Could such a half-dead man have rolled away a heavy stone and made his way unaided back to Jerusalem?

Both the stolen-body and coma theories involve a tacit acknowledgement that Jesus' tomb was empty. But the empty tomb never has been considered by the Christian community to be the best evidence of the resurrection.

It is quite clear in the Gospels that the disciples themselves never would have been convinced by the empty tomb alone, that Jesus had returned to life. They believed in the resurrection only because they saw Jesus and talked with him, not once, but on numerous occasions following his death.

The oldest written record of Jesus' appearance to his disciples is found in a letter which the Apostle Paul wrote to the church in Corinth about A.D. 56. In it he catalogued the people who had seen the risen Jesus: First, Peter; then all the Apostles; then 'more than 500 of his followers at once, most of whom are still alive . . .'

The last phrase is tremendously significant. Paul was prepared to rest his claim on the testimony of several hundred eyewitnesses who were alive and available for questioning at the time he wrote.

But even eyewitness reports can be discounted or explained away as mass hallucination. This diagnosis of hallucination may be convincing when the people involved are nervous, highly-strung, imaginative types.

But the disciples were exactly the opposite. These farmers, fishermen and tax collectors were so devoid of imagination that Jesus often had to explain his parables to them before they could grasp the point.

In the Gospels, the risen Jesus does not awe his disciples with the kind of psychic razzle-dazzle that mediums love to produce for their clients. He sits down and eats a piece of fish to let them see that it's really him, not a ghost.

The ultimate evidence of the resurrection, of course, is the existence of the Christian Church.

The centrality of the resurrection story to Christian faith was most forcefully expressed by the Apostle Paul.

'If Christ has not been raised from the dead, then we

have nothing to preach, and you have nothing to believe,' he told Corinthian Christians. 'If Christ has not been raised, then your faith is a delusion . . . more than that, we are shown to be lying against God, because we said of him that he raised Christ from death.

'But the truth is that Christ has been raised from death.'

To a modern generation that has rediscovered Jesus, the resurrection has a special significance.

As an event unique in history, it is God's warranty to mankind that Jesus was on the level.

He was what he claimed to be – not some kind of a nut.

Those are really the only alternatives, you know. As the late C. S. Lewis pointed out, it is 'patronizing nonsense' to speak of Jesus as a 'great human teacher'.

Consider some of the things he did and said. He claimed power over nature – power to heal sickness, calm storms, turn water into wine. He blithely told people, 'Your sins are forgiven,' outraging pious Jews who considered this a blasphemous usurpation of a right belonging solely to God. He spoke of God as his Father, and used an Aramaic term, 'Abba', which has the same familiar, intimate overtones as our English 'Dad'.

He said: 'I am the way; I am the truth; and I am the life; no one comes to the Father except by me.'

Shortly before his arrest and crucifixion, one of his disciples, beginning to feel nervous and doubtful, pleaded for a vision of God to bolster his sagging faith.

'Have I been all this time with you, and you still do not know me?' Jesus replied. 'Anyone who has seen me has seen the Father. Believe me when I say that I am in the Father and the Father in me; or else accept the evidence of the deeds themselves.'

A man who says things like that cannot be categorized as a great human teacher. Either he was paranoid – clean out of his head – or he was, in fact, the Most Special Messenger ever sent from God to man.

Since we're sometimes arrogant enough to think scepticism is a discovery of our generation, and that men of all previous cultures were hopelessly naïve and gullible, it is important to note that Jesus' disciples were by no means sure, when they saw him nailed to the cross, which alternative to believe. In fact, they must have leaned towards the cynical one, for they fled into hiding to save their own lives.

Yet, three days after they saw him dead, they saw him alive – not a ghost, but a living person with a recognizable body, capable of doing such very mundane things as eating a piece of broiled fish, one whose wounds could be touched and examined.

If it really happened – and the eyewitnesses cheerfully endured martyrdom rather than deny the reality of the event they witnessed – its significance is clear. It was not just a stunt proving that God can resuscitate a corpse: no first-century Jew doubted that possibility.

The significance lay – and lies – in the fact that God saw fit to do so – *in this one instance*.

It is not the fact of the resurrection, but its uniqueness that Christians ought to stress at Easter. For it was in the resurrection, as Paul said in his letter to the Romans, that Jesus was 'declared Son of God by a mighty act'.

CHAPTER THIRTEEN

And now . . .

Jesus continued his resurrection appearances among his disciples long enough to remove any shadow of doubt from their minds that they might be suffering hallucinations. 'For forty days after his death', says the Book of Acts, 'he showed himself to them many times, in ways that proved beyond doubt that he was alive.' During this period, Jesus gave his disciples what still is the great mission of the church – to spread the good news to 'every living creature'. And he promised them, 'I will be with you always.'

He did not mean he would be with them physically. One day, he led them out of the city towards the Mount of Olives. 'He raised his hands and blessed them,' Luke says. 'As he was blessing them, he departed from them and was taken up into heaven.'

This event, traditionally known as the ascension, was depicted by medieval artists in terms of Jesus being borne aloft by a cloud. This concept is, of course, untenable in the Space Age. We know that heaven is not a place 'up yonder' in the sky. Heaven is where God is – beyond all dimensions of space and time. The point of the story of the ascension is not that Jesus performed a spectacular stunt of levitation. It was simply a matter of his teaching his disciples, as he so often did, with action rather than words, that they could no longer count on his visible, tangible, corporeal presence among them.

But he had promised: 'I will be with always.' And he kept that promise. As Jesus had instructed them to do, the disciples returned to Jerusalem. They kept in close touch with one another, meeting daily in various homes or at the Temple. One day, when they were gathered together, 'suddenly there was a noise from the sky which sounded like a strong wind blowing, and it filled the whole house where they were sitting'.

This event, traditionally called Pentecost, also may be described as the birthday of the Church. For it was on Pentecost that the disciples, hitherto frightened and uncertain, experienced an extraordinary change in themselves. They *felt* God's presence among them and within them. It filled them with courage, wisdom, love and power to do many things they could never have achieved on their own. Jesus had returned – this time not in the body of a man who could be in only one place at a time, but as a Spirit who could be everywhere at once, a Spirit who dwelt within the heart and minds of men, to guide, enlighten, uplift and strengthen them. This Spirit – which the early Church soon began to call 'The Holy Spirit' – was of course invisible. But its presence was experienced by the disciples as something unquestionably real, indeed the most real thing they'd ever encountered.

Empowered and emboldened by the Holy Spirit, the disciples went forth to preach the good news throughout the known world. Often they were heard gladly – and Christian churches were soon springing up all over the Roman Empire and even in Rome itself. But they also encountered harsh persecution, at first from Jewish authorities, later from Roman emperors. Some of them cracked. But countless thousands died as martyrs, cheerfully surrendering life rather than deny their Lord.

Nineteen centuries later, the Christian church stands encrusted with age and tradition, imprisoned at times by anachronistic verbal formulations of the great truths it is charged with preaching to mankind, often stuffy and unreceptive to new insights, new forms of worship, new duties, and sometimes woefully disposed to look upon its mission as merely providing a chaplaincy to the *status quo*.

But throughout its long history, the church has had a curious way of putting out vigorous shoots of new growth just at the time when it seemed moribund. And we are witnessing another example of this miracle of renewal today. Throughout the world, people of all ages, and particularly the young, are rediscovering Jesus and claiming him as their guide to life. Best of all, they do not stop with reading and hearing *about* Jesus. They insist on getting to know him personally. And of course, that is just as possible today as it has been for all ages since the day of Pentecost. Through the power and presence of the Holy Spirit, Jesus still dwells among men and women as guide, friend, and companion. There are many ways in which you can encounter him – or rather, become aware of the fact that he's always been beside you, waiting for you to recognize him and admit him into your life.

Awareness of Jesus may develop through loving service to others . . . through the companionship of others who know him . . . through reading about him in the Bible and other books . . . through participation in the public worship and sacraments of the church . . . and especially, through prayer.

I will offer you an even more specific recommendation. Begin *every* day of your life with a brief prayer: 'Lord Jesus, please make yourself better known to me. Come into my life. Take charge of it and use it as you see fit.'

If you say that prayer patiently and persistently – and really mean it – some incredibly wonderful things will happen to you.